EMOTIONAL INTELLIGENCE

HOW TO MANAGE YOUR EMOTIONS AND THE EMOTIONS OF OTHERS

BY PATRICIA A CARLISLE

Introduction

I want to thank you and congratulate you for choosing the book, *"EMOTIONAL INTELLIGENCE: HOW TO MANAGE YOUR EMOTIONS AND THE EMOTIONS OF OTHERS "*.

In its simplest and most concise form emotional intelligence (referred to emotional intelligence as EI, or emotional quotient as EQ) is the ability to identify, use, understand, and manage your own emotions in positive ways to relieve stress, communicate effectively, empathize with others, overcome challenges, and defuse conflict. This ability also allows us to recognize and understand what other are experiencing emotionally. This recognition and understanding is, for the most part, a nonverbal process that informs thinking, and influences how well you connect with others.

Emotional intelligence differs from how we think of intellectual ability, in that emotional intelligence is a learned not acquired. This learning can take place at any time in life so the social and emotional skill set, known as emotional intelligence, is something we can all have.

People who are considered to have high EI can solve a variety of emotion-related problems accurately and quickly. They can correctly perceive emotions in faces of others, and what the emotions convey. For instance, they know that angry people can be dangerous, happy people want to relate with others, and sad people often prefer to be alone.

High EI people are also adept at managing their own as well as others' emotions. they know how to use emotional episodes in their own lives to promote specific types of thinking. Solving problems requires less cognitive effort for those with a high EI. These individuals also tend to be higher in verbal, social, and other intelligences. They are generally more open and agreeable, and are drawn to occupations involving social interactions such as teaching, counseling and interacting with others. To learn more about emotional intelligence continue reading this book.

Thanks again for choosing this book, I hope you enjoy it!

Patricia A. Carlisle, MSW, CBT

Patricia Carlisle- A Master Social Worker and a Cognitive Behavioral Therapist (CBT) gives out an expression of how important it is for an individual to take into consideration the concept of self-assessment to know what human, technical and conceptual skills they posses to perform or to achieve what they desire, or to deal with everyday life. However, every particular group of people has their own unique set of ideas, traditions and events including the frame of mind according to which people perform but there are many who faces problems and fail to maintain a healthy mind set affecting their behaviors and performance to those around them.

People like Patricia Carlisle are among those who have felt this urge of serving people and helping them out of their mental crisis towards a healthy life. She has experienced some close encounters in her personal life regarding mental health issues in her family and friends that has encouraged her to pursue this as her career.

Currently Patricia Carlisle is serving as a Certified On-Line Cognitive Behavioral Therapist with an extensive 15years of experience using Cognitive-Behavior Therapy Techniques. She envisions a world where everyone gets mental health treatment with no mental health stigma and to make it real she has already set up her own Holistic Measure Online Comprehensive Behavioral Healthcare Company after retiring from The Nord Center in The Partial Hospitalization Program (PHP) Dept for 5 years and Murtis H. Taylor Mental Health Center as a mental health counselor, psychological support technician and case manager for 10 years to emulsify her skills more professionally. Along with this, she has wrote down her passion as a clinician in 25 or more short books to help individuals and families get their life back, freeing them of the restraints of negative thinking, anxiety and depression by using different approaches. She is highly appreciated among her clients for her flexibility and professionalism of dealing with them graciously.

To reach her, make use of her direct website address: http://therapist2013.wix.com/e-therapy . As she is ready to inspire hope and contribute to health and well-being by providing the best online health care through comprehensive practice, education and research.

TABLE OF CONTENT

Chapter 1

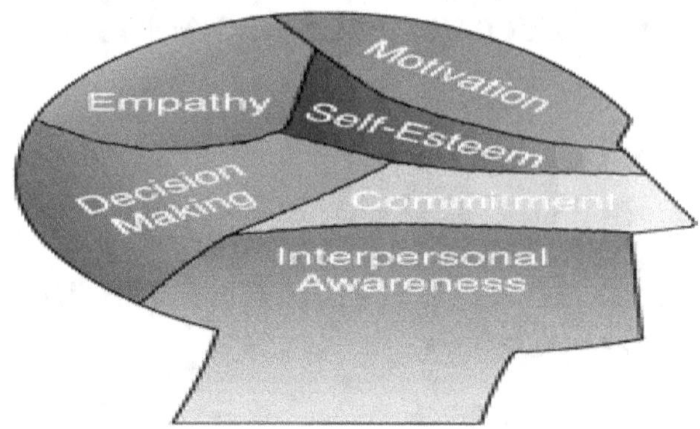

ELEMENTS OF EMOTIONAL INTELLIGENCE

Emotional Intelligence can be divided into 'Personal' and 'Social' competences, which broadly split between personal and interpersonal skills on skills you need. Within each of these sections are a range of skills which are the elements of emotional intelligence.

Personal Skills or Competences

There are three areas of personal skills or competences in emotional intelligence.

1. Self-awareness

Self-awareness encompasses:

- Emotional awareness

- Accurate self-assessment

- Self-confidence

Self-awareness is the skill of being aware of, and understanding your emotions as they occur and as they evolve. It is wrong to think of emotions as either positive or negative.

Instead, you should think of them as appropriate or inappropriate.

For example, anger is usually associated with being a negative emotion. However, it can be a completely reasonable and appropriate emotion in certain circumstances – emotional intelligence allows us to recognize our anger, and understand why this emotion has occurred.

Effective self-assessment of feelings and emotions will help to improve your confidence and self-esteem.

2. Self-regulation or Self-management

Self-regulation includes:

- Self-control

- Trustworthiness

- Conscientiousness

- Adaptability

- Innovation

Having learned to be aware of your emotions, the skill of self-regulation relates to managing them appropriately and proportionately.

Self-management skills relate to the emotions you are feeling at any given time or in any given circumstance, and how well you manage them. Self-control is a fundamental part of this, but other aspects relate to what you then do: Whether you behave in a way which is recognized as 'good' or 'virtuous' or not.

3. Motivation

The final personal skills aspect of emotional intelligence is Motivation.

Self-motivation includes our personal drive to improve, achieve, and have a commitment to our goals. Also, be initiative, and have a readiness to act on opportunities.

Self-motivation and personal time management are key skills in this area. Do not make unreasonable demands on yourself, learn to be assertive rather than just saying, 'Yes' to the demands of others.

Social or Interpersonal Skills or Competences

Interpersonal skills are the skills we use to interact with other people. They enable us to communicate appropriately and build stronger, more meaningful relationships. Emotional intelligence includes how we understand others and their emotions, and our actions and behaviors towards them.

There are two key aspects.

1. Empathy

Empathy is an awareness of the needs and feelings of others both individually and in groups, and being able to see things from the point of view of others.

Empathy helps us to develop a stronger understanding of other people situations.

It includes understanding others, developing others, having a service orientation, leveraging diversity, and political awareness.

Empathy can often be difficult to achieve. Learn to listen effectively to both the verbal and non-verbal messages of others, including body movements, gestures and physical signs of emotion. Use questions to find out more about other people and what they are feeling, and feedback to clarify that you have correctly understood their feelings. Acknowledge and respect the feelings of others even if you disagree, and avoid making comments or statements that are judgmental, belittling, rejecting or undermining.

2. Social Skills

Social skills encompasses a wide range of relationship and interpersonal skills. These range from leadership through to influencing and persuading, managing conflict, as well as working in a team.

The term 'social skills' covers a wide variety of skills and competencies, many of which are rooted in self-esteem and personal confidence. By developing your social skills, being easy to talk to, being a good listener, being sharing and trustworthy, you also become more charismatic and attractive to others.

This in turn improves self-esteem and confidence which makes it easier for positive personal dialogue, and a greater understanding and acceptance of your own emotions.

<u>Chapter 2</u>

BREAKING DOWN THE 10 EMOTIONAL TYPES

Let's spend some time analyzing 10 universal emotions that many of us tend to experience throughout our lives.

Before jumping into an explanation of each one of these emotions, it's important to understand that these emotional responses are a signal to your conscious brain that something is not working, and therefore something needs to change. They are in essence a call-to-action directing you to do something specific to alleviate your discomfort or pain.

Finally, all the emotions I am going to be discussing in this chapter are a result of stuck in a state of mind that we bring upon ourselves throughout the day.   These states are patterned responses to events, people and circumstances that have their own physiological responses, words, phrases, etc. They are in essence comfort seeking mechanisms that we use whenever things don't go our way, or as we had expected.

Let's now break down each of these ten emotional states.

DISCOMFORT

Discomfort is an uncomfortable emotion that often leads to boredom, distress, impatience or embarrassment.

You are experiencing discomfort because you are interpreting a situation or a set of circumstances in a specific way that naturally leads you to the feeling of discomfort. It's actually within this interpretation that discomfort grows. This therefore means the moment you transform or change your interpretation of the situation, is the moment you gain control over your emotional experience.

If you ever experience the emotion of discomfort it's important to first determine what it is that you are doing, and secondly how exactly you are interpreting your experience of reality. If what you are doing is not getting you the results you are after, then simply try taking a different approach. If however you are not able to tackle the situation from a different perspective, then try to change your perspective of the situation. Either way, you should be able to find an answer that will help you to pull yourself out of this uncomfortable emotional state.

If for example you are bored, then attempt to do something different with your time. Or you can simply try and interpret your experience in a unique way by turning things into a game. Either strategy will work well as long as you are willing to be flexible in your approach.

FEAR

Fear is often a very debilitating emotion that leads to worry, anxiety and indecision.

You are experiencing fear because you are interpreting a situation or a set of circumstances in a specific way that naturally leads you to the feeling of fear. This feeling of fear often results from an emotional response of what might occur in the future if you make a specific decision or take a specific action. This is all well-and-good if it's something that is based on hard facts, and evidence that is designed to protect you from harm. However, many times our fears are riddled with inaccuracies that confuse and mislead us. Therefore the first step you must always take to begin the process of removing fear from your life is to evaluate the "real" from the "imagined".

Fear is of course a very valuable emotion because it protects us from harm if we are running away from a saber-toothed tiger. However, most of the time, in this modern day-and-age, it actually harms us because it keeps us away from achieving our goals and objectives.

There are two ☐uick things you must do that will help you manage your fears more effectively. The first is to clarify what it is you really want. And the second is to prepare thoroughly for the actions you will take to achieve your desired outcomes. These two steps are critical, because the vast majority of our fears are based on a lack of knowledge and a lack of preparation. If you successfully mark both of these boxes, then you will have the ammunition you need to overcome just about any fear that you can possibly experience in our modern age.

HURT

The emotion of hurt tends to leave us feeling powerless, and often leads to a sense of loss and jealously.

You are experiencing hurt because you are interpreting a situation or a set of circumstances in a specific way that naturally leads you to feeling hurt. Likewise, feeling hurt could be a result of not communicating your needs effectively to others. As such, you must begin today by communicating what you need from your relationships in a clear and non-threatening manner.

If communicating your needs to others doesn't work, then take into consideration your expectations. Maybe your expectations are not reasonable, maybe they have changed over time, or maybe they simply no longer apply to your current relationship, and therefore may need to be reevaluated.

Finally, feelings of hurt sometimes result from a lack of understanding about our relationships or about our circumstances. In such instances, it helps if you replace your hurt with fascination and curiosity. By becoming curious, you immediately begin asking better questions, which expands the way you think, and leads to answers and possibilities that you may not have considered before.

ANGER

Anger has a tendency to spin us out-of-control, and can often lead to resentfulness.

You are experiencing anger because you are interpreting a situation or a set of circumstances in a specific way that naturally leads you to the experience of anger. However, anger can actually serve us if we are able to understand its underlying meaning.

Before you are quick to embrace the emotion of anger, it's important to understand that anger often arises because one or more of our rules has been violated by others. As such, we become angry because we no longer feel in control of the situation, people or circumstances. In such instances we can actually let go of anger quite quickly, by spending some time reevaluating our rules. Maybe they're not reasonable, or they are out-of-date, or just maybe they shouldn't be applied in these circumstances.

Alternatively, anger can come about because of an incorrect interpretation of circumstances or people's intentions. In such instances you must question whether or not you have possibly misinterpreted the situation, or simply misinterpreted the person intentions. In that case, be open to the possibilities and passionately look for alternative meanings. Only an open and flexible approach will provide you with the answers you are after.

GUILT

Guilt has a tendency to leave us feeling somewhat deflated, and can often lead to the emotion of regret.

You are experiencing guilt because you are interpreting a situation or a set of circumstances in a specific way that naturally leads you to the feeling guilt. And the longer you hold onto that guilt the worse it tends to get as it continues to fester and grow inside your head.

When experiencing guilt it's important to remember that our experience of guilt is simply our interpretation of what we did or failed to do, and the impact that this has had on others. The moment you choose to interpret the events and circumstances of your life in a new and unique way, is the moment that guilt suddenly changes, and turns into something that can potentially motivate and empower you to take positive action.

Realize that the impact that your actions have had on others may not be as they seem. Therefore in such instances you may need to take a look at your rules for feeling guilty. Maybe these rules need to be reassessed.

Finally, guilt is often resolved when you are able to make peace with yourself, and with the people you may or may not have hurt.

FRUSTRATION

Frustration is one of those emotions that we just love to hate because it makes us feel as though we're so close, yet so far away from the outcome we want.

You are experiencing frustration because you are interpreting a situation or a set of circumstances in a specific way that naturally leads you to feeling frustrated. Yet it is within this feeling that your answers lie.

You are frustrated because you are trying to do something, however you don't seem to be getting the results you are after. It's like you're being held-back from your goal by some outside force that you can't seem to control.

Instead of trying to control the situation, the key is to begin thinking outside the box; to begin thinking of new possibilities, ideas and possible solutions that might help you solve the problem you are dealing with. And sometimes all it takes is for you to look for new information that will provide you with the insight you need to see the circumstances from a slightly different perspective.

Finally, frustration often results from not getting the results you are after. In such instances all it takes to resolve your frustrations is to simply change your approach; try something new and different that you hadn't considered before. Curiosity, determination, and a flexible approach are the keys you should be looking for.

INADEQUACY

Inadequacy can make you feel miserable, unworthy and incompetent. It's an emotion that leaves you feeling like you're at the bottom with no way out.

You are experiencing inadequacy because you simply don't have the experience, skills or knowledge to live up to your high expectations. So you can either change your expectations about yourself and your ability, or you can go out there and gain the necessary knowledge, skills and experience necessary to achieve the outcomes you desire to have in your life.

You could also be experiencing inadequacy because you are simply undermining your own strengths and abilities. In such circumstances it's always important to get a second opinion. Therefore, go out there and ask someone for feedback. Ask them to give you their honest observations. Maybe they will provide you with some very surprising insights and perspectives.

Finally, inadequacy can often stem from a lack of confidence. If you you are riddled with low self-esteem, then it seems perfectly okay to feel inadequate. However, if you take the time to build your confidence, you will likewise develop more self-belief, and will begin to feel better about yourself and your prospects.

OVERWHELM

Feeling overwhelm is one of those emotional feelings that creeps up on you over time, and before you know it, it takes over your life, and can at times lead to the very debilitating emotions of grief and depression.

You are feeling overwhelm because you may have too much on your plate or you are simply unable to manage or take control over an aspects of your life.   In such circumstances you feel out-of-control, and unable to respond accordingly.

The solution to feeling overwhelm lies in taking back control over small chunks of your life, one piece at a time. It means taking a part of your life, and dividing it up into smaller manageable pieces that you can successfully work with. It also means letting go of any unnecessary obligations and commitments that are weighing you down, or simply rescheduling them in a way that will free up your time while providing you more space to do what's most important.

Overcoming overwhelming feelings is simple if you know what to do and are committed to taking the actions necessary to reschedule and re-prioritize your life accordingly. Sometimes all it takes is a little lesson in productivity.

DISAPPOINTMENT

Disappointment is the feeling of not getting what you want, and often stems from a sense-of-defeat.

You are experiencing disappointment because you are interpreting a situation or a set of circumstances in a specific way that naturally leads you to feeling disappointed.   Instead of looking for solutions and answers, you;re stuck within a muddy pit full of unfulfilled goals, objectives, and dreams that never became reality.

Whenever we experience disappointment, we always wish that things could have been different. However, no matter how hard we try, we can't change the past, although we can alter our experience of the past in a positive way.

Instead of wallowing in disappointment, choose instead to learn from your experiences so that you can better yourself in the future. At other times, it's even worthwhile to look for opportunities that might now be available as a result of the disappointment that you have just experienced.

Disappointment can often be a result of having unrealistic high expectations that can almost never be realized. In that case, change your expectations by lowering them to a level that can be realistically achieved. This could very well dig you out of the dreaded pit of disappointment.

Finally, disappointment is simply a result of having an unfulfilled goal. If that's the case, then you might need to adjust your goals in order to make them more achievable. That way you are less likely to feel disappointed.

LONELINESS

Loneliness can be a very debilitating emotion that can lead to sadness and stagnation.

You are experiencing loneliness because you are seeing your life through a lens that separates you from everyone and everything else that lies outside of you. This is no way to live life given the fact that there are so many opportunities to connect with others on a daily basis.

The key to overcoming loneliness is to reconnect with others, to reconnect with your environment, and to reconnect with a higher cause that will help you feel more fulfilled and passionate about your life.

- Make an effort to talk to someone.

- Make an effort to listen to someone.

- Make a contribution to your community.

- Spend time in the environment.

- Play with a baby or pet.

Go out there and help someone in need. Your help may be all they need to help them feel a little less lonely.

Finally, loneliness grows in the heart because we tend to forget about all the things that we are grateful for. It's this gratitude that will help you restore the balance you are sorely missing. And it's this gratitude that will encourage you to open your heart to others.

HOW TO MANAGE YOUR EMOTIONAL STATE

You should now be very much ready and prepared for any emotional surprises that life throws your way. However, there may still be instances where unexpected circumstances could push you into limiting patterns, and habits that could potentially create emotional turmoil, and throw you off course. In such instances, you need to learn to manage your emotional state a little more effectively, and it is this process that we will discuss here.

BUILDING YOUR EMOTIONAL FORTRESS

In order to strengthen your resilience during tough times, it is

worthwhile to spend some time building your emotional fortress.

Your emotional fortress is a place you go-to in your mind that keeps you strong during tough and difficult times.

To build your emotional fortress close your eyes and imagine a special place that only you know about. This is your personal sanctuary that will help you find strength and guidance. This place could be a valley, a mountain, along the beach, a special room, a house, or any other place that gives you strength during difficult times.

Within this emotional fortress you can talk with your peers and mentors. These are the people who inspire and help strengthen you during difficult times. They are there to help and guide you through any emotional struggles you might be experiencing.

Your emotional fortress also contains a number of self-improvement resources that you can use to help strengthen and resolve your issues. All of these resources and support networks are there for you to help you gain the upper-hand whenever you are facing difficulties.

You should use your emotional fortress in times of great emotional difficulty where you require that extra support to help steady and point you in the right direction. Therefore, instead of reacting emotionally in limiting ways to the events and circumstances in your life, take some time to remove yourself from your circumstances and step into your emotional fortress, which will help provide you with the answers and guidance you need to respond in positive ways.

PSYCHOLOGICAL TRANSFORMATION

Your thoughts, expectations, self-talk, and perceptions all work together to create the reality you experience on a daily basis. Moreover, they all come together and influence the emotions you experience at any moment in time.

You must therefore choose your thoughts consciously, and your self-talk wisely, and change your expectations of events and circumstances in positive ways making them work for you rather than against you.

The types of seeds you plant in your mind grow throughout the day. For better or worse, they will influence your perceptions of reality. You must therefore choose seeds that will promote positive emotional growth to help you make the most of your day, and the opportunities that are presented before you.

CONTROL YOUR BREATHING

Whenever you are feeling emotionally under the weather, it's always important and very helpful to calm yourself by breathing consciously. Simply, breathe-in for five counts, and exhale for five more counts, while maintaining your concentration purely on your breathing.

Undertake this process for up to five minutes at a time, and you will quickly find a new vigor and energy that you can use to help you think more clearly, and effectively about the circumstances you are being confronted with.

COMMUNICATE YOUR NEEDS AND DESIRES

One very effective way to avoid emotional turmoil is to simply communicate your needs and desires to others.

Many times our communication is very poor, which leads to misunderstandings and conflicts. This results in emotional turmoil and mayhem. To resolve this, simply ask others how they feel, why they are feeling that way, and how they would like to potentially resolve these feelings. Likewise, communicate your needs in the same way.

Sometimes all it takes is open communication and a willingness to listen, to resolve any emotional conflict that you might be experiencing throughout your day.

PHYSIOLOGICAL TRANSFORMATION

I have discussed above how our psychology influences how we feel throughout the day. Well, the same is true of our physiology.

How you use your body, what you do with your body, and how you position your body has a significant impact on the emotions you experience throughout the day.

For instance, whenever you feel the emotion of anger, take a look at your body and determine how it is responding, what it is doing, and how it is changing as your anger escalates.

Compare this angry state to a time when you are feeling calm, sociable and relaxed. What does your body do, and how does it respond in such instances?

You will quickly find that your body responds quite differently to each emotional state that you encounter throughout the day. This therefore raises the question of whether changing how your body moves and positions itself can influence how you feel emotionally from moment-to-moment?   And the answer to this question is a resounding YES!

ANCHORING

Here you are putting yourself into a peak emotional state of the type of emotion that you would like to experience while anchoring it to a part of your body.

Say for instance, I would like to anchor the emotion of passion to my body. I would think of times in the past that I have felt passionate about something. then I would live through these experiences in my head until the moment I have passion running through my veins. At this moment at the peak of the emotion I would anchor this passionate state to a part of my body. This could simply mean squeezing my thumb or earlobe.

Once the anchor has been set, I can trigger the emotional state of passion at any time throughout the day by squeezing my thumb or my earlobe to get me out of a bored emotional state.

EYE MOVEMENTS

Finally, it's important to point out that in many ways our emotions are actually linked to the movement of our eyes. This means that when we are experiencing a certain emotion our eyes are moving in a certain and specific way that signals to the brain that we are now (for instance) experiencing the emotion of depression.

Without needing to go into any detail here, the next time you are experiencing a limiting emotional state try experimenting with this, and begin moving your eyes in unpredictable ways. I'm confident that you will quickly find that the emotional state you were just experiencing has somewhat dissipated.

Chapter 3

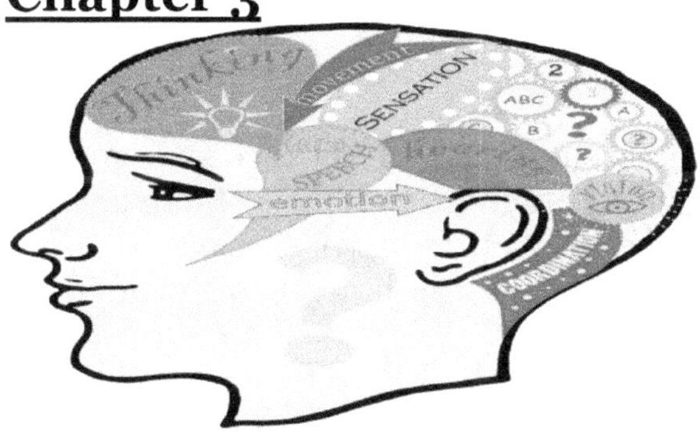

SIGNS THAT YOU LACK EMOTIONAL INTELLIGENCE

When emotional intelligence (EQ) first appeared to the masses, it served as the missing link in a peculiar finding: People with average IQs outperform those with the highest IQs 70 percent of the time. This anomaly threw a massive wrench into the broadly held assumption that IQ was the sole source of success.

Decades of research now point to emotional intelligence as being the critical factor that sets star performers apart from the rest of the pack. The connection is so strong that 90 percent of top performers have high emotional intelligence.

Emotional intelligence is the "something" in each of us that is a bit intangible. It affects how we manage behavior, navigate social complexities, and make personal decisions to achieve positive results.

Despite the significance of emotional quotient (EQ), its intangible nature makes it very difficult to know how much you have, and what you can do to improve if you're lacking.

1. You get stressed easily

When you stuff your feelings inside, they quickly build into the uncomfortable sensations of tension, stress and anxiety. Unaddressed emotions strain the mind and body. Your emotional intelligence skills help make stress more manageable by enabling you to spot and tackle tough situations before things escalate.

People who fail to use their emotional intelligence skills are more likely to turn to other, less effective means of managing their mood. They are twice as likely to experience anxiety, depression, substance abuse, and even thoughts of suicide.

2. You have difficulty asserting yourself

People with high emotional quotient (EQ) balance good manners, empathy, and kindness with the ability to assert themselves and establish boundaries. This tactful combination is ideal for handling conflict. When most people are crossed, they default to passive or aggressive behavior. Emotionally intelligent people remain balanced and assertive by steering themselves away from unfiltered emotional reactions.   This enables them to neutralize difficult and toxic people without creating enemies.

3. You have a limited emotional vocabulary

All people experience emotions, but it is a select few who can accurately identify them as they occur. Research shows that only 36 percent of people who do this, which is problematic because unlabeled emotions often go misunderstood, which leads to irrational choices and counterproductive actions. People with high EQs master their emotions because they understand them, and they use an extensive vocabulary of feelings to do so. While many people might describe themselves as simply feeling "bad," emotionally intelligent people can pinpoint whether they feel "irritable," "frustrated," "downtrodden" or "anxious."   The more specific your word choice, the better insight you have into exactly how you are feeling, what caused it, and what you should do about it.

4. You make assumptions quickly

People who lack EQ form an opinion ☐uickly and then succumb to confirmation bias, meaning they gather evidence that supports their opinion, and ignore any evidence to the contrary. More often than not, they argue, ad nauseam, to support it. This is especially dangerous for leaders, as their under-thought-out ideas become the entire team's strategy. Emotionally intelligent people let their thoughts marinate, because they know that initial reactions are driven by emotions. They give their thoughts time to develop, and consider the possible consequences and counter-arguments. Then, they communicate their developed idea in the most effective way possible, taking into account the needs and opinions of their audience.

5. You hold grudges

The negative emotions that come with holding on to a grudge are actually a stress response. Just thinking about the event sends your body into fight-or-flight mode, a survival mechanism that forces you to stand up and fight or run for the hills when faced with a threat. When a threat is imminent, this reaction is essential to your survival, but when a threat is ancient history, holding on to that stress wreaks havoc on your body, and can have devastating health consequences over time.   In fact, researchers at Emory University have shown that holding on to stress contributes to high blood pressure and heart disease. Holding on to a grudge means you're holding on to stress, and emotionally intelligent people know to avoid this at all costs. Letting go of a grudge not only makes you feel better, but can also improve your health.

6. You don't let go of mistakes

Emotionally intelligent people distance themselves from their mistakes, but they do so without forgetting them. By keeping their mistakes at a safe distance, yet still handy enough to refer to, they are able to adapt and adjust for future success. It takes refined self-awareness to walk this tightrope between dwelling and remembering. Dwelling too long on your mistakes makes you anxious and gun shy, while forgetting about them completely makes you bound to repeat them. The key to balance lies in your ability to transform failures into nuggets of improvement. This creates the tendency to get right back up every time you fall down.

7. You often feel misunderstood

When you lack emotional intelligence, it's hard to understand how you come across to others. You feel misunderstood because you don't deliver your message in a way that people can understand. Even with practice, emotionally intelligent people know that they don't communicate every idea perfectly. They catch on when people don't understand what they are saying, adjust their approach, and re-communicate their idea in a way that can be understood.

8. You don't know your triggers

Everyone has triggers situations, and people that push their buttons and cause them to act impulsively. Emotionally intelligent people study their triggers and use this knowledge to sidestep situations and people before they get the best of them.

9. You don't get angry

Emotional intelligence is not about being nice; it's about managing your emotions to achieve the best possible outcomes. Sometimes this means showing people that you're upset, sad or frustrated. Constantly masking your emotions with happiness and positivity isn't genuine or productive. Emotionally intelligent people employ negative and positive emotions intentionally in the appropriate situations.

10. You blame other people for how they make you feel

Emotions come from within. It's tempting to attribute how you feel to the actions of others, but you must take responsibility for your emotions. No one can make you feel anything that you don't want to. Thinking otherwise only holds you back.

11. You're easily offended

If you have a firm grasp of who you are, it's difficult for someone to say or do something that gets your goat. Emotionally intelligent people are self-confident and open-minded, which create a pretty thick skin. You may even poke fun at yourself or let other people make jokes about you because you are able to mentally draw the line between humor and degradation.

Bringing It All Together

Unlike your IQ, your EQ is highly malleable. As you train your brain by repeatedly practicing new emotionally intelligent behaviors, it builds the pathways needed to make them into habits. As your brain reinforces the use of these new behaviors, the connections supporting old, destructive behaviors die off. Before long, you begin responding to your surroundings with emotional intelligence without even having to think about it.

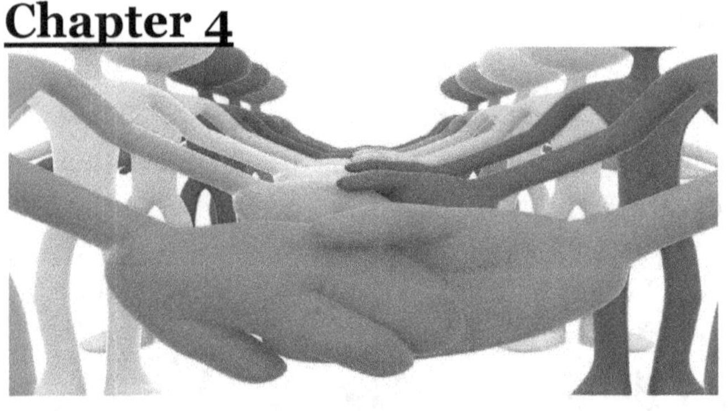

Chapter 4

UNDERSTANDING AND MANAGING YOUR EMOTIONAL TRIGGERS

When you react badly to an event, it is common to blame the event for your reaction e.g. your boss asks you to work overtime and you get angry. Your natural reaction may be to blame your boss for your anger. However, you may notice that other people, when asked to work overtime, do not always react angrily. In fact, some just accept it, and get on with it while others, if it is not convenient, inform their boss they will not be able to work overtime.

For just about every possible event, you have your own beliefs, feelings or views. In the example above, you may feel that you cannot say 'No' to your boss. Alternatively, you may feel that your boss should not be asking you to work overtime because you work long enough hours. Can you see how either of these beliefs would cause you to react angrily when your boss asks you to work overtime?

Now imagine if rather than these beliefs, you believed that you had the right to say 'No' to your boss; or you just accepted that from to time you would have to work overtime. Can you see how these beliefs would lead to you feeling differently about the situation? As a result, you would be less likely to get angry.

Your beliefs about a situation are just one way that emotional triggers can influence your behavior. Sometimes, emotional triggers can lead to positive behavior; however, emotional triggers often lie behind some of our worst behavior. If you are unaware of your emotional triggers, these negative behaviors can seem automatic, and out of your control. Fortunately, as you become aware of your emotional triggers and start to monitor them, you realize that you have the opportunity to intervene in the space between the event and your response, thus creating a more desirable situation.

Taking control of your emotional triggers

You can implement the following steps to help you take control of your emotional triggers by increasing your awareness and developing new ways of responding. These steps are divided in to 2 phases understanding your emotional triggers, and managing your emotional triggers.

Understanding your emotional triggers

1. Identify your emotional triggers

A trigger is an experience that draws us back into the past, and causes old feelings and behaviors to arise. It is important to note that the emotional trigger is not always the specific situation. In the example given earlier the emotional trigger is probably not the fact that you are being asked to work overtime. The following are just some of the emotional triggers which are more likely to be the issue in that particular example:

- Being asked to do something you do not want to do.

- Taking orders from authority figures.

- Having someone else control your time.

- Lacking the confidence or assertiveness to say 'No'.

Thinking errors – e.g. you may believe that the boss always expects you to be the one to work overtime, and never asks anybody else

As you can see, each of these emotional triggers is different and would have to be dealt with using a different approach. That is why it so important to observe your feelings and emotions to find the exact emotional triggers which are leading to your undesired behavior.

2. Spot external stimuli

Some triggers are situational and social. Take note of the situations where you behave in the undesired manner. Include the people who were there, what was happening etc. In time, you will begin to see a pattern which will better enable you to identify the root cause of the issue.

3. Identify internal causes

When you find yourself behaving in the undesired manner, take note of your thoughts and feelings. Your thoughts and feelings about situations, and people, heavily influence your behavior. In many cases, these thoughts and feeling are inaccurate, unhelpful or no longer relevant. When you become aware of them, you are in a position to challenge them.

4. Accept that we all have emotional triggers

We are all human and as such, we are all fallible. Having emotional triggers which cause you to behave in a negative way does not make you a bad person. Instead, view them as an opportunity to grow and develop into an better person.

Managing your emotional triggers

5. Keep a journal

The best and simplest way to monitor your behavior is to keep a journal. Whenever you behave in the undesired manner, make a record of your thoughts, feelings, emotions, and the situation you were in when the behavior took place. Note what's going on in your head and in your surroundings at the time. Be as detailed as you can be.

Tracking your triggers is the first step in mastering them. It allows you to identify patterns, and pinpoint the causes of your behavior. When you can do this, you are then in a position to make changes.

6. Challenge yourself

The key to change is placing yourself in difficult positions and being open to doing something new and more constructive. Many people avoid their problems, but avoidance is not an effective problem solving strategy. If you want to change your behavior, you must challenge yourself. It is not always easy, but the rewards are always worth it.

7. Come up with alternatives

If you want to change your behavior, it is not enough to simply stop behaving that way. That approach is rarely effective. You need to substitute a new behavior. Brainstorm new strategies you can use instead of the old behavior e.g. if you do not want to do the overtime, commit yourself to becoming more assertive so that you can tell your boss that you will not be available. You may need to develop and implement new skills.

8. Know your capacity

Proceed at your own pace. To continue with the previous example; if you want to be more assertive, you can start out by being more assertive with your spouse and friends if you need to practice before talking with your boss. This will build your confidence, and as you see that the world does not end when you say 'No', you will build a greater resolve to stand your ground.

9. Take time to relax

Taking the time to manage your stress levels will help you to manage your emotions better. Identify the behaviors which help you to de-stress and fit them into your schedule on a daily basis. As you begin to de-stress and unwind, you will find that you become more resilient and determined.

10. Live healthy

Another way to make yourself more resilient is to take good care of your body and mind. Eat right, sleep well and exercise regularly. You'll be better prepared to bounce back from any obstacles that may arise.

11. Develop a strong support network

When you're dealing with stubborn issues, it's good to know you have people who care about you and want to help. By telling people whom you can trust about your desire to change, you will have a support network whom you can turn to during your tough times, and with whom you can celebrate your progress. The knowledge that you are not alone while on your journey can be enough to give you the courage to keep going.

When you behave in an unacceptable manner, it is easy to blame others or to blame events for your behavior. When you blame outside factors it may make you feel better in the short-term, but in the long-term you are cheating yourself of the opportunity to live a happy, healthy life.

If you are behaving in an inappropriate or undesirable way, the problem may be due to emotional triggers. We all have our own unique emotional triggers. Learning to handle them constructively enables us to fix the issues that get in our way and move ahead in life. So, rather than blame outside factors for your unwanted behavior; take it on the chin, accept that you need to make some changes, and get to work. When you implement the steps outlined above, you will be well on the way to taming your emotional triggers, and enjoying a happy and healthier life.

Chapter 5

HOW TO USE EMOTIONAL INTELLIGENCE TO IMPROVE YOUR TIME MANAGEMENT

If I were to ask you about your best technique to wisely manage your time, you would probably share a routine you follow at work or home. You might start listing tactics like, "Do the hardest task early in the day," or "Only check emails three times a day." I'd be willing to wager you wouldn't say, "I manage my emotions well."

I know what you're thinking... "What in the world does that have to do with how I manage my time?" The truth is, so much of managing your time is about managing your energy. And while physical energy is important, your mental and emotional energy are also essential in giving you the motivation, and clarity to work on the tasks that will give you the greatest sense of accomplishment.

If you're looking for a fresh strategy to managing your time more effectively, consider how well you are doing in these four areas of emotional intelligence:

Self-Awareness

The focus here is on recognizing and understanding your moods, emotions, and what drives you. Do you notice how different tasks impact your desire to work on the next item in your day? When possible, do you plan your day by alternating activities that add or take away your mental or emotional energy? And do you reflect on the larger purpose for which you are completing your tasks?

Self-Management

Ever looked at the next item in your day and felt overwhelmed or anxious? Here's the bigger question: How did you handle the impulse to work on something else?   Self-management is all about recognizing disruptive impulses and controlling them. So instead of choosing to check your email to avoid a difficult task, you choose to break down the task into more manageable steps. Or you remind yourself of more difficult tasks you've undertaken lately at which you were successful to gain more confidence.

Social Awareness

For this area, think empathy. How good are you at recognizing the emotions of other people? If your job requires you to make requests of other people to get your work done (and most do), do you stop and reflect on how the request will make them feel? Most importantly, does that knowledge or insight change the way you frame the request? We've all experienced a leader or supervisor who seemed to be blind (or unconcerned) to our emotional state, and how it impacted our motivation to accept the task and/or complete it well.

Relationship Management

For leaders and managers who want to use their time well, this area of emotional intelligence is critical. Your best work comes from the full engagement of every team member. And the only way you can get that level of engagement is to know how to communicate with them in a way that connects with them on both a mental and emotional level. So, if you're looking to take your time management skills to the next level, maybe you should stop trying to figure out how to squeeze another hour out of your day. Start spending a little more time reflecting on how your emotions are increasing or decreasing the energy you need to actually get the right work done.

Chapter 6

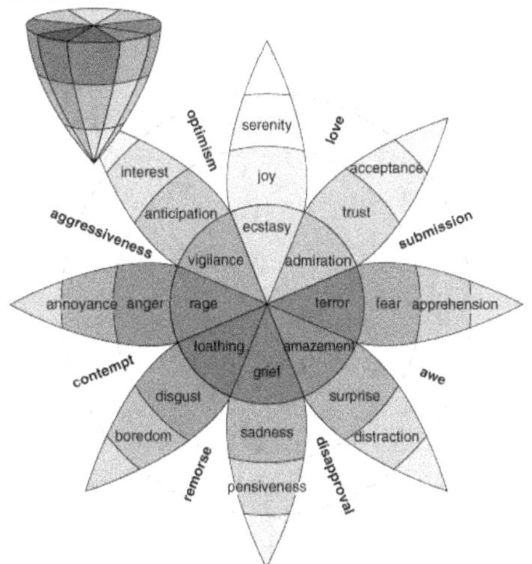

18 TIPS ON HOW TO CONTROL YOUR EMOTIONS

Each individual is driven by emotions, and they have the power to dictate one's actions. So, managing your emotions is like developing a skill or a habit.

When you act on emotions that are misinformed or an unhealthy reaction to a particular situation, you often end up regretting your actions.

Potent negative emotions like anxiety, embarrassment, fear, envy or anger can quickly get out of control once they have been triggered. If you let these emotions dominate your daily life, they can become deep-seated, and arise more frequently.

The first step toward managing your emotions is to understand them. They need to be handled with logic and a sense of control.

Here are a few steps to help you effectively control your emotions.

1. Avoid situations that trigger negative emotions

If you can't control your emotions, then control the situation. Avoid circumstances that trigger unwanted emotions. For example, if you feel anxious and stressed around a certain colleague, figure out a way to keep your distance from that person. However, if your find yourself increasingly avoiding people or situations, and it begins to interfere with your daily life, use other techniques to deal with your emotions.

2. Remove yourself from the situation

When you think you are in a situation in which you cannot control your emotions, and you may lash out in an inappropriate manner, simply excuse yourself if you can. Find a private place where you can unleash your negative emotions.

3. Breathe and calm yourself down

If you cannot excuse yourself from a situation that is triggering your emotions, turn your attention to your breathing. Count your breaths in your mind, as this will help you stay focused and keep your mind off the negative emotion. Deep breathing will also help you calm down.

If you are at all provoked to speak, you can tell the person, 'We will talk about it later.' Intense feelings usually diminish within a short period of time.

4. Be aware of your emotions

Once you have calmed down, try to identify your feelings. If you are not aware of the times when you are emotional or overreacting, it will be hard to manage your emotions. Naming your emotions will help you recognize them. If you feel envious, angry or sad, label the feeling in your mind. Be honest and admit it to yourself. As you identify your emotions, keep track of them to help you identify triggers and areas to work on improving.

5. Analyze why you feel the way you do

After identifying your feelings, explore the reasons why you feel the way you do and what triggered it. Ask yourself, 'What's wrong? What is causing you to feel this emotion?' Most of the time, the way you think about a situation can cause you to feel the way you do. Understand your feelings, rather than defending or expressing them.

6. Modify your expectations

Take a look at your expectations. If they are not realistic, you are bound to be disappointed or stressed. For instance, if you expect your house to be clean and organized all the time, even a little mess can destroy your peace of mind. So, adjust any expectations that are unrealistic, and accept things that you cannot change.

7. Change the way you think about a situation

Once you know the root of the problem, you can change the way you think about it. Your thoughts and beliefs shape your feelings. So, consider your thoughts. Are they based on truth? Are they logical? Are your beliefs true? If you start thinking about the situation differently, you will start feeling better. The more you understand your emotions, the more they will start to diminish.

8. Choose the way you react

Managing your emotions is a skill that you need to develop with discipline. and continuous effort until it becomes a habit. If you cannot do anything to change your thoughts, change your response to emotional triggers. When you are anxious or angry, control your emotion and take deep breaths. This will calm you down.

9. Avoid negative thinking

When you are in an emotional turmoil, it's easy to get caught in a negative thought pattern. You tend to replay the situation and experience the feelings again. Break out of negative thinking. There are several tricks and techniques you can use to help you do this.

For instance, put a rubber band on your wrist and when you find yourself thinking negatively, snap the rubber band. This will serve as a physical reminder to work to control your emotions. Another thing you can do is consciously replace negative thoughts with positive ones. Think of something positive that will make you feel happy – it could be a place you love or someone who makes you happy.

10. Shift your focus

Shift your attention from things or people who trigger your emotions. If you suffer from low self-esteem, stop focusing on people who you think are superior to you. When you focus too much on others, you are putting yourself in center stage, and constantly comparing yourself to them. This will always tend to make you unhappy. Instead, focus on people and situations that make you feel confident about your abilities.

11. Change your mood

Do something different. Change your mood by doing something that makes you feel good instantly. For instance, if you feel bored and sad, change your mood by going for a walk in a new neighborhood or catching up with friends who you haven't seen for a long time. Close your eyes and imagine yourself to be relaxed and comfortable.

12. Think of the future

Remember your anger, disappointment or hatred might seem real and important right now, but those feelings will be gone in a month, a week or a few days. Intense emotions make you momentarily forget about the future. Don't let your emotions dictate your actions. When you are angry, ask yourself, 'What would be the consequences of my actions? How will I feel tomorrow when I look back at this?' Look beyond the moment and see the bigger picture. This will help you relax.

13. Don't react impulsively

 Reacting immediately based on your emotions can be a mistake that you end up regretting later. Oftentimes, what you say or do during such an emotional outburst makes things worse instead of better. So, the next time you notice yourself getting angry, pause, take a deep breath, and consider the situation. Stop your impulse to react. Continue breathing until you calm down. Tell yourself that this is temporary.

14. Find a healthy outlet for your emotions

Emotions should never be bottled up. Find a healthy way to release your feelings. Talk to someone you trust about the situation. A different perspective may help. Writing down your thoughts and feelings on a daily basis can help release and take the power out of your emotions. Mindfulness meditation or mantra meditation is calming, and relaxing for some, while exercises like kickboxing or martial arts does the trick for others.

15. Write it down

 Set aside a few minutes every day to journal your thoughts. Journaling helps you come to know yourself by revealing your innermost fears, thoughts and feelings. While you write, ask questions about your emotions and feelings. This will help you understand them more clearly.

16. Force yourself to think

Your emotions can make you blind and cause you to react stupidly. Rather than being objective and rational, your emotions may make you become sloppy. When you feel out of control, force yourself to think. For instance, when you start feeling angry at something, try to remember the details of your first date. This will help subdue your emotional response.

17. Learn from others

Observe how others handle their emotions. Notice how they deal with their frustrations and disappointments. Ask them, 'How do you keep calm when you feel angry or anxious?' You can apply their insights and strategies to deal with your emotions.

18. Forgive yourself and others

Your emotional triggers could be your friends, colleagues, boss, family members or even yourself. You may feel sudden surges of anger when you think of something in the past that you could have done differently or someone does something that you despise. The key here is to forgive yourself or the other person for what has occurred, and thereby lessen the power of your triggers. When you forgive, you detach yourself from the negative emotions.

Chapter 7

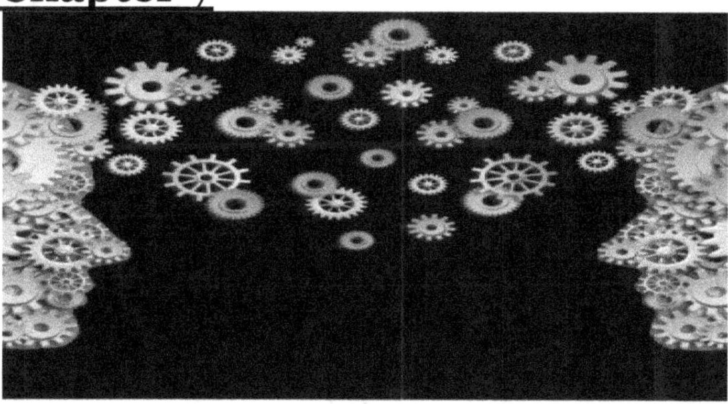

HOW TO BECOME EMOTIONALLY INTELLIGENT

In a world that frequently favors speaking over listening, and thinking about oneself over others, it's really hard to pay attention to our own emotions, or the emotions of others. But if you don't, you'll miss out on the valuable information emotions can teach us, and the meaningful relationships you can build as a result. Emotional intelligence is a form of social intelligence. Someone who has high emotional intelligence is able to recognize and monitor their own and others' feelings and emotions, to engage with and navigate them, and to use that emotional information to guide their own thinking and action.

I like to think of emotionally intelligent people kind of like detectives. Every time they interact with someone, they're able to uncover the emotional pieces that are missing from what a person actually says out loud. Then, they're also able to use that emotional information in an effective way, like to become a better manager, a better teammate, or a better friend.

There are many, long-lasting benefits to making efforts to increase your emotional intelligence. First, studies have shown that emotional intelligence can be more important than raw skill in many cases. Perhaps most importantly, having high emotional intelligence can help you create and maintain more meaningful relationships both at work and in your personal life.

The good news is, no matter your personality and emotional tendencies, there are things you can do to increase your emotional intelligence. Here is a list to help you understand how.

1) Observe your own emotional tendencies

Not only can emotionally intelligent people sense the emotional needs of others, but they also know themselves very well because they're able to understand, manage, and effectively express their own feelings. You can only learn to manage your own emotions if you learn to recognize them in youself.

This is easier said than done, of course. Start by going on with your day, and paying attention to how you feel, and what specific situations make you feel that way. What's your emotional state when you wake up in the morning? How about when that guy cut you off at an intersection on your way to work? Or when your coworker brought you a cup of coffee and remembered how you like it? How about when your boss rejected your idea in front of your coworkers?

Next, ask yourself how all these feelings connect with your behavior. Throughout the day, did they impact your communication with others, your productivity, or your overall sense of well-being? The better you become at recognizing and understanding your emotions and behavioral impulses, the better you'll be at managing them.

2) Don't judge yourself

As you become more and more aware of your emotions, you might find you're judging yourself for them especially when experiencing a negative emotion, such as anger or sadness. But remember: Every emotion you have, positive and negative, is a useful piece of information that can teach you something about your own needs and preferences.

If you're quick to judge how you're feeling, you'll have a lot of trouble being honest with yourself about how you feel, which is totally counterproductive. Allow yourself to feel those emotions so that you'll be able to better manage them and recognize them in others.

3) Learn to control your negative emotions

Managing your emotions effectively is a big part of increasing your emotional intelligence. The hardest part of this tends to be managing your negative emotions. But doing so is important, as it helps you avoid letting negative feelings cloud your judgment. This will make you a better decision-maker because you'll be able to look at a problem and find a resolution in a calm and rational way. It'll also help you become more receptive to feedback and able to use criticism to improve your performance.

The key is to let yourself feel those negative emotions, but practice deciding how to behave once you feel them. For example, let's say you're driving and someone cuts you off at an intersection. Your initial reaction may be surprise, followed by anger. But you have a choice here: You could lay on the horn and yell out the window, "Who do you think you are?," or you could shrug it off because, let's be honest, the ten seconds it added to your commute didn't really affect your day.

Remember: How you react to things is your own responsibility. If someone hurts your feelings and you react by yelling at them, then that's your own doing. They didn't "make" you yell at them it's you who makes that choice.

The next time you feel a negative emotion, take a deep breath to experience that feeling and let it wash over you. Then, take a deep breath and make a conscious decision about how you want to behave in response.

4) Learn to express difficult emotions

Part of being emotionally intelligent is knowing when to share your emotions with others. After all, being honest with others about how you feel encourages trust, and helps people feel comfortable opening up to you. It's all about choosing your moments, and sharing how you're feeling without hurting anyone.

5) Take a genuine interest in what people are saying

As you consciously observe how you're feeling, begin practicing recognizing and acknowledging how other people are feeling as well. In other words, practice empathy. Empathizing with others is one of the most powerful parts of being emotionally intelligent, and it will help you get closer to others, gain their support when you need it, and have an easier time smoothing over conflicts.

The best way to uncover how someone else is feeling is to become an active listener. This means really, truly paying attention to what people are saying. This is really difficult for a lot of people especially those who've been taught that listening and deferring to others is a sign of weakness, and that speaking is better than listening.

The first step to take an honest look at your listening skills. Are you a naturally good listener? Or do you tend to spend most of the time someone else is talking thinking about what you're going to say next? A lot of people don't know they aren't good listeners until they make a conscious effort. Then, make the dcision to listen closely and carefully in every conversation.

6) Ask relevant questions

Sometimes, all you have to do is ask. While you shouldn't jump in with questions every time your conversation partner stops talking, you should ask relevant and clarifying questions to demonstrate you've been paying attention, to show the person you're interested in the conversation, and to dig deeper into what they're telling you.

To dig deeper, you might use a questioning technique called funneling. Funneling means asking a series of questions that become more restrictive at each step. Here's an example:

"Tell me about your last week at work."

"Which projects have you spent the most time on?"

"Did you run into any challenges on those projects?"

"What have you done so far to mitigate that challenge?"

"How can I help you get closer to overcoming it?"

The first questions are open and allow for broad answers, and at each step the questions become narrower and more focused. This is a great technique for gathering a lot of information about a situation so you can put the pieces together.

7) Pay attention to body language

Body language is another clue to uncovering how someone is feeling. Everyone communicates in ways that are nonverbal, like posture, facial expressions, and body movements. When you're conversing with someone, take note of how they use their body when they speak, and treat it like the useful information it is. You might acknowledge it by saying, "I get the sense that this makes you unhappy. What's causing that?"

You'd also do well to observe how your own emotions manifest themselves in physical ways. For example, that tightening in your stomach might be caused by stress or anxiety. Those high energy levels might be an indication that you're really excited about something.

8) Take responsibility for your actions

Humility, like empathy, is a powerful part of being emotionally intelligent, and one key way to be humble is to take responsibility when you say the wrong thing or hurt someone's feelings.

Some people might think acknowledging when you did something wrong is a sign of weakness or lack of self-confidence, especially when you didn't mean to. But taking responsibility for your actions shows people you're self-aware, honest, and committed to being a team player. And, people are a lot more willing to forgive and forget if you make an honest go at making things right. In the end, this will have a positive impact in all areas of your life.

To increase your social intelligence, you'll need to practice becoming more self-aware, transparent, adaptable, socially aware, empathetic ... the list goes on. There are plenty of other ways to improve that aren't on this list, but it's a start and something you'll want to continue working on for the rest of your life. The more you practice, the more you'll reap the benefits.

9) Practice open-mindedness

In general, being narrow-minded is an indication of lower emotional intelligence. Think about it: Open-minded people are more willing to listen to other people points of view, and try to understand them by putting themselves in the their shoes. As a result, people are more willing to trust them with true thoughts and feelings because they aren't worried about being judged. Open-minded people also have a strong sense of self because they don't confine themselves by their own beliefs.

One way of practicing open-mindedness is to observe how others react to situations and compare it to how you would react in that same situation. If they react differently than you would, think about why this is and try to see it from their point of view.

As you become better with this, you'll likely find that challenging your beliefs and allowing yourself to explore new ideas will benefit you both professionally and personally.

10) Practice observing how you feel

Often we lead hectic, busy lifestyles and it's all too easy for us
to lose touch with our emotions. To reconnect, try setting a
timer for various points during the day. When the timer goes
off, take a few deep breaths and notice how you're feeling
emotionally. Pay attention to where that emotion is showing
up as a physical feeling in your body, and what the sensation
feels like. The more you practice, the more it will become
second nature.

11) Notice your behavior

While you're practicing your emotional awareness, take the
time to notice your behavior too. Observe how you act when
you're experiencing certain emotions, and how that affects
your day-to-day life. Managing our emotions becomes easier
once we become conscious of how we react to them.

12) Question your opinions

In this hyper-connected world, it is easy to fall into an 'opinion
bubble'. This is a state of existence where your own opinions
are constantly re-enforced by people with similar viewpoints.
Take time to read the other side of the story and have your
views challenged (even if you still feel they are right). This will
help you understand other people and be more receptive to
new ideas.

13) Take responsibility

Your emotions and behavior come from you, they don't come
from anyone else and once you start accepting responsibility
for how you feel, and how you behave it will have a positive
impact on all areas of your life.

14) Celebrate the positive

A key part emotional intelligence is celebrating and reflecting
on the positive moments in life. People who experience
positive emotions are generally resilient, and more likely to

have fulfilling relationships, which will help them move past adversity.

15) Reflect

Reflecting on negative feelings is just as important as reflecting on the positive. Understanding why you feel negative is key to becoming a fully-rounded individual, who is more able to deal with negative issues in the future.

16) Don't forget to breathe

Life throws various situations our way, with most of us experiencing some sort of stress on a regular basis. To manage your emotions when this happens and avoid outbursts, don't forget to breathe. Call time out and put some cold water on your face, go outside and get some fresh air or make a drink anything to keep you cool and give yourself a chance to get a hold on what's happening and how you should respond.

17) A lifetime process

Understand and remember that emotional intelligence is something you develop and requires continual improvement; it's very much a lifetime practice.

18) Look at yourself objectively

Knowing yourself completely is difficult and it's almost impossible to look at yourself objectively, so input from those who know you is vital. Ask them where your strengths and weaknesses lie, write down what they say and compare it. Look out for any patterns and remember not to argue with them – it doesn't mean they're right they're just trying to help you gauge your perception from another's point of view.

19) Keep a diary

A great way to get an accurate gauge of yourself is to keep a diary. Start by writing down what happened to you at the end of every day, how it made you feel and how you dealt with it. Documenting details like these will make you aware of what you're doing, and will highlight where problems might come from. Periodically, look back over your comments and take note of any trends.

20) Understand what motivates you

Everyone has a core motivation when they begin a project. The difficulty is keeping this driving force in mind when adversity appears. All too often people start a project, but fail to complete it because they lose their motivation to do so. Take time to understand what motivates you, and use it to push you across the finish line.

21) Take it easy

Sometimes emotional outbreaks occur because we don't take the time out to slow down and process how we're feeling. Give yourself a break and make a conscious effort to meditate, do yoga or read – a little escapism works wonders. And then the next time you have an emotional reaction to something, try to pause before you react.

22) Acknowledge your emotional triggers

Self-aware individuals are able to recognize their emotions as they occur. It's important to be flexible with your emotions, and adapt them to your situation. Don't deny your emotions stage time, but don't be rigid with them either, take the time to process your emotions before communicating them.

23) Predict your feelings

Think about a situation you're going into and predict how you will feel. Practice naming and accepting the feelings - naming the feeling that puts you in control. Try to choose an appropriate reaction to the feeling rather than just reacting to it.

24) Trust your intuition

If you are still unsure about which path to take, trust your intuition. After all, your subconscious has been learning which path to take throughout your entire life.

25) Snap out of it

One key way to keep your emotions in check is to change your sensory input – motion dictates emotion as the old saying goes. So jolt your physical body out of routine by attending an exercise class or try channeling your busy mind with a puzzle or a book - anything to break your existing routine.

26) Maintain a schedule (and stick to it!)

Ensuring that you create a schedule and stick to it is extremely important if you want to complete tasks effectively.

When you schedule appointments in your calendar, you're saying to yourself: "I'm going to do A, B, and C by X date and it's going to take Y hours."

Once you make this promise, it becomes harder to procrastinate."

27) Eat well

This sounds like an easy one, but regulating what you eat and drink can have a massive effect on your emotional state, so try your best to maintain a balanced diet.

28) Don't get mad

Funnel your emotional energy into something productive. It's okay to keep overwhelming emotions inside, especially if it's not an appropriate time to let them out. However, when you do, rather than vent it on something futile, turn it into motivation instead. Don't get mad, get better.

29) Be interested

A key factor in managing yourself and your emotions is consciously taken the time to be interested in the subject matter, whether it be business or personal.

30) Don't expect people to trust you (if you can't trust them)

Establishing trust with a person can be difficult, and once it's lost it's very hard to regain. Try to be mindful that people are only human and will make mistakes. By offering your trust, you are inviting people to offer their trust in return.

31) It's your choice

You have the ability to choose how you react to a situation - you can either overreact or remain calm. It's your choice.

32) Personal goals

Personal goals can provide long-term direction and short-term motivation. So grab a pen and paper and think about where you want to be, and set some targets for yourself. Base them on your strengths and make them relevant to you, and ultimately, make them exciting and achievable. This task alone is enough to get you instantly motivated!

33) Be realistic

When you've set a new goal, be sure to give yourself realistic and clear aims to achieving that goal and understand that change is an inevitable part of life. Achievement boosts confidence, and as self-confidence rises so does the ability to achieve more, see how it works?

34) Positive thinking

To keep motivated it's important to maintain a positive and optimistic mindset. See problems and setbacks as learning opportunities instead of failings, and try to avoid negative people and opt to surround yourself with positive, well-motivated people they'll have a great effect on you.

35) Lifelong learning

Both knowledge and information are key for feeding your mind and keeping you curious and motivated. And with information so easily accessible, you have the opportunity to fuel your values and passions at the click of a button!

36) Be prepared to leave your comfort zone

The biggest barrier to achieving your full potential is not challenging yourself frequently enough. Great things can happen to you if you're willing to leave your comfort zone, so do so as often as you can.

37) Help

Don't be afraid to ask for help when you need it, and vice versa. If others need help, don't hold back in giving it to them. Seeing other people succeed will only help to motivate yourself.

38) Stand and stretch

For an instant short term boost to your motivation, take a stand and stretch out as far as you can for 10 seconds. When you return to your desk, you'll be in the correct frame of mind and ready to work.

39) Listen

Before you're able to empathize with someone you first need to understand what it is they're saying, which means listening is at the very core of empathy. It involves letting them talk without interruption, preconceptions, skepticism, and putting your own issues on pause to allow yourself to absorb their situation, and consider how they are feeling before you react.

40) Try to be approachable

Whether you're the leader of a team or working on a project with others, try to remain accessible and approachable.

41) Perspective

We're all familiar with the phrase "put yourself in their shoes", and this is exactly that. The simplest way of gaining a little perspective the next time an issue or situation arises is to switch places with the other person, and think about what's happening from their point of view. Sometimes there's no right or wrong, but at least you'll understand enough to help them to resolve the issue or offer give them some useful advice.

42) Open yourself up

One of the quickest ways to offer a sincere exchange or sign of empathy is to listen to someone's experiences and connect to it with a similar experience of your own. Don't be afraid to open yourself up, it might just be the start of a great and lasting friendship.

43) Experience new culture

The old saying 'travel broadens the mind' is still true, even in this ever shrinking world. Sometimes the best way to open your mind is to jump on a plane and go somewhere completely different.

44) Cultivate a curiosity about strangers

Highly empathetic people have an insatiable curiosity about strangers. When we talk to people outside of our social circle we learn about them, and begin to understand opinions, views, and lives that are different from our own. So next time you sat on a bus you will know just what to do.

45) Acknowledge the other person

Another useful tip is, listening to what a person has to say, use acknowledgement words such as 'I understand' and 'I see' to show a person you're listening, (but of course only say these things if you are actually listening!).

46) Get started

A good way to get started on improving your social skills is to isolate one skill you know you'd like to develop, this narrows it down and gives you focus. Internationally known psychologist, studies show that highlighting someone you know to be good at that particular skill, observing how they act and how they control their emotions, and applying that knowledge to yourself.

47) Walk in someone else's shoes

Not literally of course! Everyone has heard the phrase 'walk a mile in someone else's shoes', but how many people actually practice this advice? Give it a try, you never know.

48) Practice makes perfect

The idea of practicing your social skills might sound strange, but like everything in life, practice makes perfect.

49) Face-to-face

We don't mean to sound old, but taking your social life offline and engaging face-to-face with people will open up so many opportunities for you to gain and develop insite of that person! Emotional intelligence doesn't expand within the confines of social media.

50) Start networking

A good way to practice your social abilities is to attend local networking events. The great thing about these events is that everyone attending has a shared reason for attending.

51) Body language

We're talking about the importance of nonverbal communication and how that can affect a person's opinion of you. Body language, tone of voice and eye contact is key to letting others know how you feel emotionally. So once you've got your emotions intact, think about how you're physically coming across.

52) The unknown

The ultimate method to building your social skills is to get out there and be sociable. It sounds simple, but you can't strengthen your social skills without being social! Join a group or network outside of your circle; it's the perfect way to put all of our tips into play.

WHAT TO AVOID

Those with a high EQ very rarely display the following traits:

53) Drama

Emotionally intelligent people listen, offer sound advice, and extend empathy to those who need it, but they don't permit others' lives and emotions to effect or rule their own.

54) Complaining

Complaining implies two things – one, you are a victim, and two, there are no solutions to the problems. Rarely does an emotionally intelligent person feel victimized, and even more infrequently do they feel a solution is beyond their grasp. So instead of looking for someone or something to blame, they think constructively and dissolve the solution in private.

55) Negativity

Emotionally intelligent people have the ability to curb cynical thoughts. They acknowledge that negative thoughts are just that – thoughts – and rely on facts to come to conclusions as well as being able to silence or zone out any negativity.

56) Dwelling on the past

Those with high emotional intelligence choose to learn from the mistakes and choices they have made, and instead of dwelling on the past they are mindful to live in the now.

57) Giving in to peer pressure

Just because everyone else does something, you don't have to follow suit if you don't want to. Think independently, and never conform just to please other people.

58) Being overly critical

Nothing destroys a person's morale faster than being overly critical. Remember that people are only human and have the same motivations (and limitations) as you. Take the time to understand another person then communicate to them the changes you would like to see.

By understanding and successfully applying emotional intelligence, you too can reach your full potential and achieve your goals.

59) Selfishness

While a degree of selfishness is required to get ahead in life, too much can fracture relationships and cause disharmony. Try to avoid being overly selfish and consider other's needs.

Chapter 8

HOW TO DEAL WITH YOUR FRIENDS EMOTIONS

Difficult conversations can raise awkward feelings. Here's how to manage.

Here are tips for handing some of your friends emotions:

1. Crying

Crying is a natural physiological response when someone feels hurt, disappointed, sad, or had expectations that weren't met. It could be a result of stress or a buildup of disappointments. Allow a person to take a moment when tears come to their eyes. Calmly wait for them to signal they are ready to move on. Generally, if you tell a person to take his or her time and calmly sit in silence, he or she will let you know when they're ready to move on. If you have a tissue available, offer it. If the crying is uncontrollable, offer to reschedule the discussion, but only as a last resort. This is for the other person's benefit: It is always better to give someone a moment to regroup than to make them feel bad for crying.

2. Embarrassment

When a person sees or feels that he or she has been acting or believing in a way that has been harmful to himself or others, he may feel embarrassed. Do not try to alleviate or soften the reaction. Allow him a moment to catch his breath. When you sense you can move on, ask him to articulate what he has now discovered or learned before asking about what action he might take. Articulating a learned lesson helps a person feel stronger.

3. Defensive Anger

Defensiveness and anger usually subside after the initial response if you don't fuel the fire. So stay calm. When you sense someone's anger, you might reflexively defend yourself, get angry in return, or you shut down. Of course, if you feel you are at risk of being harmed, you should find a way to remove yourself as soon as possible. But if there is no risk, understand that the person's display of anger could be a natural reaction to information they didn't want to hear. Whether she is mad at herself or others, give her a moment to express herself. Let her vent to release the steam. Then when she starts to calm down, see if you can't help look at the cause of her anger and sort out the truth from the speculation. Then maybe you can find some ways of dealing with the situation so she gains even a small sense of control. If the anger doesn't subside, you might ask for another meeting when the person is emotionally prepared to look at solutions with you.

4. Confusion or Fear

When you face these feelings, listen to the person's stories so you can discover what is holding them back. Do not try to diffuse or soften their emotions, or even tell them it is understandable to feel afraid; it is better to say that you would like to understand what's causing the fear so you can help them move forward with confidence. Then withhold your judgment when they respond. You may have to encourage them to speak by asking a few questions that show you are curious, and that you care. If you do, it is more likely they will open up. Most people want to be listened to and understood. Listening with compassion will help them build their courage, and once the emotions start to dissipate, see if you can't help them discover the roots of their emotions. What do they feel they have lost, or are afraid they will lose, based on the situation? Is the loss real or their imagination? Do they need to take the first step forward?   If they are ready to explore with you, this is the best way to help.

HOW TO HELP OTHERS MANAGE THEIR EMOTIONS

You can help those around you become more emotionally intelligent. But before you help others you must master your emotion. An important tool for helping others manage their emotions is "resonance."

For example, put two tuning forks of the same pitch side by side. As you strike the first, you can notice that the second starts vibrating. In a relationship, each individual acts like a tuning fork that receives and transmits emotional waves. When one person has an emotional reaction, the "vibrations" affect the other who starts vibrating in response. This response cycles back and intensifies or dampens the first person's emotion.

If the two people are emotionally reactive, they will escalate their negative interactions into a frenzy. If one of them stays centered, she can start a dampening cycle even when the other person stays reactive.

When you master your emotions, you can bring equanimity to any relationship. If you can stay grounded in the midst of an emotionally charged situation, you can help others stay conscious. On the other hand, unless you master the emotional skills I described in the previous chapters, you cannot help others.

FIVE COMPONENTS OF SELF-MASTERY

RECOGNITION

Although you can't observe the internal states of others, you can observe external signs. Emotions have a physical component (flushing cheeks), and a behavioral component (tightening fists). You can make valid statement about other's feelings based upon these observations (physical and behavioral), an understanding of the other's situation; empathy, and your attribution of values and objectives to others.

It is important to realize that what you feel others think is not what they may actually think and feel. You can't read another person mind. On the other hand, disregarding emotional signs is a great disadvantage. The skillful way to work with attributions is base on the best evidence available, state them tentatively, and ask the other person to verify them.

For example, if you notice a team member is sitting with crossed arms, completely quiet, and distant from others, you could say, "Tim, I see that you're quiet, your arms are crossed, and you're seated far from everyone else. I'm wondering how you're feeling about our conversation." Notice how different that is than attacking Tim with "Why are you upset? What's wrong with you?"

ACCEPTANCE

To work with someone emotions it is necessary to accept them without judgment. It's not only useless to get upset about what he or she feels, it's also counterproductive. You might feel the urge to tell a troubled co-worker to cheer up, or tell your child that things are not really so bad, but this may never work. The other person may not only continues to feel troubled, but now they feel alienated as well.

For example, a manager who notices that employees are scared about an upcoming organizational change might feel inclined to reassure them, "There's nothing to be concerned about." He may mean well, but his statement can scare the employees more. Challenging others' emotions makes them feel judged, misunderstood, and disrespected. In extreme cases, it can make them doubt their sanity.

DEFUSION

Nothing defuses emotions like your own relaxed stance. Simply not reacting shows a dampening effect on intense emotions. Accepting the other person emotions without judgment helps them become focus. Even in extreme circumstances it is possible to defuse the other's emotions. Someone may be very upset with you, but you don't have to escalate the conflict. You can take responsibility for what you triggered in the other person, and do your best to maintain focus. With a open conversation, you can allow the other person to express their feelings and thoughts fully. When you understand the story behind the emotion you can take appropriate action to address it. Without a reaction, an attack can't last long. Like a fire that runs out of fuel, the emotional heat will consume itself. That's why the best way to receive another person emotions is with empathy, without judgment or argument. In order to defuse aggressive energy, look for ways to agree with the individual; don't concern yourself with how incorrect you may believe the other person statement may be. Look for the slightest grain of truth which you can agree to disagree.

<u>Conclusion</u>

Thank you again choosing this book!

Working on your emotional intelligence is the most important aspect of your personal development.

Research has shown that people with higher levels of emotional intelligence enjoy more satisfying and successful careers and relationships.

If you work on ways to enhance your emotional intelligence, you are likely to become more charismatic, interesting, and attractive to others; and you will also give your self-esteem a boost.

Remember, you are always in full control of your emotions no matter how things may appear. And you can always choose to feel differently and take control of your emotional state. Therefore no one is to blame, but yourself, because emotions come from inside-out, and not from the outside-in.

Finally, if you enjoyed this book, then I'd like to ask you for a favor, would you be kind enough to leave a review for this book on Amazon? It'd be greatly appreciated!

Thank you and good luck!

Preview Of 'SUCCESS: UNDERSTANDING INADEQUACY AND HOW TO OVERCOME THOSE FEELINGS OF INADEQUACY'

Chapter 1

WAYS TO COMBAT INADEQUACY

Let's take a look at some ways to deal with feelings of inadequacy. A good way to combat inadequacy is to think about all of the things you can do. Then think about the things that you can do well, or better than others. You should always be able to remind yourself of how special you are to the world.

Therefore, keep a journal or album of accomplishments, and awards you have achieved. This will be a good reference for you whenever you need to remind yourself of what you are capable of.

Next, after you bring to mind all of the things you can do, think of how, what you do well can prosper you. Why not allow one of your talents to bring you into a fortune, or at least make you a living? How fun would it be to do something you enjoy while getting paid for it? Try to find a way to put your skill or talent to use where it can be a blessing to you and others at the same time. This will be a constant reminder to you of how special you are to society because of your ability.

Encouraging others is another great way to cope with feelings of inadequacy. When you are encouraging others, you are not thinking about yourself. Instead, you are focused on pushing others toward their dreams, and making them feel great while doing so. In turn, the inspiration you give to other will come back to you.

An excellent way to defeat feeling inadequate is to not spend a lot of time alone. Instead, spend time with people so that you always have someone else to think about other than yourself. Some great ways to keep from being alone are to live with someone, volunteer regularly for a charity, or join a sports league. Having continuous company will keep you thought of, and keeps you in the presence of someone to reach out to.

A great way to stay away from thinking negatively about yourself is to stay away from negative environments. Do not spend your time in a place, or environment where bad things take place. Instead, spend your time in places where you can grow, and be encouraged as great things take place.

As you can see, there are multiple ways to overcome with feelings of inadequacy. Therefore, know that you are special, and let nobody, including yourself tell you any differently.

To check out the rest of (SUCCESS: UNDERSTANDING INADEQUACY AND HOW TO OVERCOME THOSE FEELINGS OF INADEQUACY) go to Amazon.com

Check Out My Other Books

Below you'll find some of my other popular books that are popular on Amazon and Kindle as well. Alternatively, you can visit my author page on Amazon to see other work done by me.

OVER 600 POSITIVE AFFIRMATIONS THAT WILL CHANGE YOUR LIFE.

INSECURE: Stop the Insecurity and Learn how to Overcome Jealousy and Build Self-Esteem.

LETTIONG GO: Learn How to Embrace the Future

MINDSET: HOW YOU CAN BECOME POWERFUL AND ACHIEVE SUCCESS ON YOUR TERMS.

A GUIDANCE TO MENTAL TRAINING: LEARN HOW TO DEVEOP MENTAL RESILIENCE.

BOUNDARIES In Relationships: How to develop boundaries in MARRIAGE and DATING

FAILURE IS NOT AN OPTION: LEARN HOW TO OVERCOME THE FEAR OF FAILING.

ASSERTIVENESS: HOW TO STAND UP FOR YOURSELF AND BE STRONG IN EVERY SITUATION

COMMUNICATION SKILLS AND TECHNIQUES FOR DUMMIES.

BONUS: SUBSCRIBE TO THE FREE BOOK

Beginners Guide to Yoga & Meditation

"Stressed out? Do You Feel Like The World Is Crashing Down Around You? Want To Take A Vacation That Will Relax Your Mind, Body And Spirit? Well this Easy To Read Step By Step

E-Book Makes It All Possible!"

Instructions on how to join our mailing list, and receive a free copy of "Yoga and Meditation" can be found in any of my Kindle eBooks.

NOTES

NOTES

NOTES

NOTES